JAROSLAV PONCAR

TIBET PANORAMA

Text by Iris Lemanczyk

EDITIONPANORAMA

TIBET

Der Wind pfeift. Es ist kalt, obwohl die Sonne schon seit Stunden scheint. Blau, Grau, Grün und Weiß herrschen hier oben vor. Andere Farben scheinen in der Weite des tibetischen Hochplateaus nicht zu existieren. Das intensive Blau des Himmels, die graue Mondlandschaft aus Steinen, Sand und Steppe, dazwischen einzelne grüne Wiesen, dahinter das Weiß der schneebedeckten Gipfel des Himalaja. In der dünnen, kristallklaren Luft scheint dies alles zum Greifen nah. Kein Dunst zeichnet die Umgebung weich. Jede Farbe, jede Kontur, jedes Detail zeigt sich in ungebrochener Klarheit, scharf abgesetzt vom tiefblauen, fast unendlich weiten Himmel. Tibet, das Schneeland. Das Dach der Welt. Kein Wunder, denn Tibets Durchschnittshöhe liegt bei mehr als 4 500 Metern. Es ist das höchstgelegene Land der Welt, dem Himmel am nächsten und besteht zu gut zwei Dritteln aus kaum besiedelten Steppen- und Berggebieten.

Lha Gyal lo – die Götter mögen siegen, rufen sich die Tibeter fröhlich zu, sobald sie einen der zahllosen Gebirgspässe überwunden haben. Lha Gyal lo. Der über 5 000 Meter hohe Pass ist erreicht. Tenzin Rintschen, der sich auf seiner ersten Pilgerreise befindet, knüpft seine Gebetsfahne an die vielen anderen, die bereits im schneidenden Wind flattern. Seine Begleiter stapeln einige Steine auf die Pyramiden aus Geröll, die vorangegangene Reisende und Pilger aufgetürmt haben. Lha Gyal lo. Jetzt ist es nicht mehr weit zu ihrem Ziel, dem Kailash, dem heiligsten Berg Asiens. Der Kailash, das Schneejuwel.

TIBET

The wind howls. The air is cold, although the sun has already been shining for hours. At this height, the only colours to be seen are blue, grey, green and white. No other colours appear to exist in the vastness of the Tibetan mountain plateau. The intense blue of the sky, the grey moon landscape of rock, sand and steppe, interspersed here and there by green meadows, and behind them the white of the snow-capped peaks of the Himalayas. In the thin, crystal-clear air, everything seems close enough to be touched. No haze softens the surrounding environment. Every colour, every contour, every detail appears in perfect clarity, sharply delineated against the deep blue, infinite expanse of sky. Tibet, the land of snow. The roof of the world. Little wonder, since Tibet's average height above sea level is nearly 15,000 ft. It is by far the highest country in the world, the closest to Heaven one might say, and consists a good two-thirds of almost unpopulated steppe and mountain regions.

Lha Gyal lo – May the Gods triumph, the Tibetans call out happily to each other as soon as they have surmounted one of the innumerable mountain passes. Lha Gyal lo. The 16,000 ft. high pass has been reached. Tenzin Rintschen, who is making his first pilgrimage, ties his prayer flag to the many others which already flutter in the cutting wind. His companions stack a few stones on the pyramids of scree piled up by previous travellers and pilgrims. Lha Gyal lo. They are now not far from their destination, the

TIBET

Le vent souffle. Il fait froid alors que le soleil brille depuis des heures. Le bleu, le gris, le vert mais aussi le blanc dominent le paysage ici sur les hauteurs. Les autres couleurs semblent avoir été éradiquées de l'immensité du haut plateau tibétain. Le bleu intense du ciel, le paysage lunaire gris de roche, de sable et de steppe avec, par endroits, quelques prairies vertes isolées, et derrière, le blanc des sommets enneigés de l'Himalaya. Tout cela semble à portée de la main dans l'air raréfié et limpide comme le cristal. Aucune brume n'adoucit les alentours. Chaque couleur, chaque contour, chaque détail tranche clairement et nettement sur le bleu profond du ciel d'une immensité presque sans fin. Le Tibet, Pays des Neiges mais aussi Toit du Monde, car il est perché à une altitude moyenne de plus de 4 500 mètres. Ce pays, le plus haut du monde et aussi le plus proche du ciel, est couvert aux deux tiers de steppes et de montagnes presque inhabitées.

Les Tibétains s'interpellent en criant joyeusement « Lha Gyal lo », victoire aux Dieux, dès qu'ils ont franchi l'un de ces innombrables cols montagneux. Lha Gyal lo. Le col, à plus de 5 000 m d'altitude, est enfin atteint. Tenzin Rintschen, dont c'est le premier pèlerinage, accroche son drapeau de prières derrière tous ceux, très nombreux, qui battent déjà dans le vent cinglant. Ses compagnons empilent quelques cailloux sur les pyramides d'éboulis édifiées par les voyageurs et pèlerins qui les ont précédés. Lha Gyal lo. Il n'est plus loin du but maintenant, le Kailash,

TIBET

Sopla el viento y hace frío a pesar de que el sol luce desde hace horas. Aquí arriba dominan el azul, el gris, el verde y el blanco. Parece que el resto de los colores se hubieran desvanecido en la inmensidad del altiplano tibetano. El intenso azul del cielo, el gris paisaje lunar que forman las piedras, la arena y la estepa; de vez en cuando, verdes pastos aislados y al fondo las blancas cimas coronadas de nieve del Himalaya. En este ambiente transparente todos los elementos del paisaje parecen al alcance de la mano. No hay vapor que difumine los perfiles. Cada color, cada contorno, cada detalle se muestra con una impresionante claridad, se distingue acusadamente del trasfondo azul del vasto, casi interminable cielo. Tibet, el país de la nieve. El techo del mundo. Y esas denominaciones no son una exageración, ya que la altura promedio del Tibet es de 4 500 metros. Es el país más alto del planeta, el más cercano al cielo y está compuesto en casi dos terceras partes de macizos montañosos y estepas prácticamente despobladas.

"Lha Gyal lo": ¡que venzan los dioses! Así se felicitan alegremente los tibetanos cada vez que han pasado algunos de los innumerables pasos de montaña. "Lha Gyal lo". Hemos alcanzado el paso de casi 5 000 metros de altura. Tenzin Rintschen, que está realizando su primer viaje de peregrinación, anuda su bandera de oración a las muchas otras que ya están ondeando en el cortante viento. Sus acompañantes apilan algunas piedras sobre las pirámides de cantos rodados que han ido formando los viajeros y peregrinos

TIBET

Il vento fischia. È freddo, benché il sole splenda già da ore. Blu, grigio, verde e bianco sono i colori che sovrastano quassù. Non sembrano esistere altri colori nella distesa dell'altopiano tibetano. L'intenso blu del cielo, il grigio del paesaggio lunare fatto di pietre, sabbia e steppa, qua e là qualche prato verde, a ridosso il bianco delle cime nevose dell'Himalaya. Nella sottile aria cristallina tutto sembra tanto vicino da poterlo toccare. Non c'è bruma che ammorbidisca il paesaggio. Ogni colore, ogni contorno, ogni dettaglio si prospettano con una chiarezza senza sfumature, risaltando nitidamente nell'azzurro carico del cielo pressoché immenso. Tibet, il Paese delle Nevi. Il Tetto del Mondo. Niente di cui meravigliarsi, visto che l'altitudine media del Tibet è poco più di 4 500 metri. È il Paese più in quota al mondo, il più vicino al cielo e per oltre due terzi composto da territori stepposi e di montagna scarsamente abitati.

Lha Gyal lo – che gli dei siano vittoriosi, esclamano gaiamente i tibetani appena hanno oltrepassato uno degli innumerevoli valichi di montagna. Lha Gyal lo. Il passo di oltre 5 000 metri è stato raggiunto. Tenzin Rintschen, che è al suo primo pellegrinaggio, annoda la sua bandierine di preghiera alle molte altre che già si agitano nel vento tagliente. I suoi accompagnatori posano alcuni sassi sulle piramidi di detriti affastellate da viaggiatori e pellegrini precedenti. Lha Gyal lo. Adesso non manca molto alla meta, al Kailash, il monte più sacro dell'Asia. Il Kailash, il gioiello di neve.

Tenzin Rintschen legt sich auf den steinigen Weg, streckt sich langsam aus, erhebt sich wieder, reckt sich, faltet die Hände über dem Kopf, an der Stirn und am Hals. Er schreitet die kurze Strecke voran, die er gerade mit seinem Körper abgemessen hat, taucht dann erneut auf den Boden. Tausende, abertausende Male auf und nieder, so wird der Pilger den heiligen Berg umrunden. Holzplatten, die er an seinen Knien und Händen befestigt hat, schützen ihn vor dem steinigen Untergrund. Die Umrundung des Kailashs gilt als symbolisches Ausschreiten des Weges vom Leben in den Tod und weiter durch das Zwischenstadium, das Bardo, in eine neue Geburt. Jede Niederwerfung reinigt den Geist und bringt Verdienste auf dem Weg zur Erleuchtung.

Tief empfundene Religiosität durchdringt das Schneeland, durchdringt die Tibeter noch heute. Selbst nach Jahrzehnten der Fremdbestimmtheit, in der die Chinesen alles versucht haben, um die tibetische Religion und Kunst auszulöschen. Am 9. September 1951 zogen 3 000 chinesische Soldaten Fahnen schwenkend in die tibetische Hauptstadt Lhasa ein. Die Hilferufe der Tibeter an die Vereinten Nationen verhallten wirkungslos. Anfangs griffen die Besatzer wenig in den tibetischen Alltag ein, doch ihre Truppenstärke wuchs und wuchs. Auf einmal richteten sie Volkskommunen ein, in denen sie die Tibeter sieben Tage die Woche zum Arbeitsdienst zwangsverpflichteten. Gleichzeitig kollektivierten die Besatzer Eigentum und Vieh der Tibeter. Jeder Widerstand wurde mit Zerstörungen der Klöster, Exekutionen, Vergewaltigung, Folter oder Deportation beantwortet. Im Februar 1959 legte der junge Dalai

Kailash, the holiest mountain in Asia. Mount Kailash, the jewel of the snow.

Tenzin Rintschen lies down on the stony path, stretches slowly, stands up again, stretches again, folds his hands over his head, across his forehead and around his neck. He steps forward the short way just measured by his body, and then lies down on the ground again. The pilgrim will circle the Holy Mountain in this way, up and down, thousands and thousands of times. Wooden tiles which he has strapped to his knees and hands protect him from the stony ground. The pilgrimage around the Kailash symbolises the passage from life into death, and on through the intermediate stage of the Bardo, into rebirth. Every act of prostration cleanses the spirit, and brings rewards on the path to enlightenment.

Even today, a deep sense of religion still permeates Tibet, this land of snow. Even after decades of foreign domination, during which the Chinese have tried everything in their power to stamp out Tibetan religion and art. On 9th September 1951, 3,000 Chinese soldiers entered the Tibetan capital of Lhasa waving their banners. Tibet's call for aid to the United Nations went unanswered. In the beginning, the occupiers interfered little in the daily life of Tibet, although the troop strength grew continuously. Suddenly they decided to establish peoples' communes, in which the Tibetans were subjected to forced labour seven days a week. At the same time, the occupiers "collectivised" the property and cattle of the Tibetans. Every act of resistance was met with destruction of monasteries, executions, rape, torture or deportation. In February 1959, the young Dalai Lama took his spiritual tests in various

le mont le plus sacré de toute l'Asie. Le Kailash ou Joyau des Neiges.
Tenzin Rintschen se couche sur le sol pierreux, s'allonge lentement, se relève, s'étire, joints les mains au-dessus de sa tête, devant son front et son cou. Il parcourt la distance qu'il vient de mesurer avec son corps puis retombe sur le sol. Il se lève et se prosterne des milliers et des milliers de fois, comme les autres pèlerins qui font la circumambulation du mont sacré. Des planchettes de bois qu'il a fixées sur ses genoux et les paumes de ses mains le protègent du sol caillouteux. Le contournement rituel du Kailash est considéré comme le passage symbolique de la vie à la mort et la traversée par l'étape transitoire, le Bardo, qui sépare la mort d'une nouvelle naissance. Chaque prosternation purifie l'esprit et le récompense sur la voie de l'illumination.
Le Pays des Neiges et les Tibétains sont profondément pieux aujourd'hui encore, même après des décennies d'oppression étrangère au cours de laquelle les Chinois ont tout tenté pour que disparaissent la religion et l'art tibétains. Le 9 septembre 1951, 3 000 soldats chinois font leur entrée dans la capitale tibétaine de Lhassa en agitant des drapeaux. Les appels à l'aide des Tibétains aux Nations-Unies se heurtent à un mur à l'époque. Au début, les occupants n'interviennent guère dans le quotidien des habitants mais l'importance de leurs troupes ne cesse d'augmenter. Ils instaurent un beau jour des communes populaires dans lesquelles ils forcent les Tibétains à travailler sept jours par semaine. Dans le même temps, les occupants nationalisent la propriété et le bétail de la population. Toute tentative de résistance est réprimée par la

que pasaron anteriormente por allí. "Lha Gyal lo". Ya no queda mucho para alcanzar su objetivo, el Kailash, la montaña más sagrada de Asia. El Kailash, la joya de la nieve.
Tenzin Rintschen se acuesta sobre el camino cubierto de piedras, se estira lentamente, se vuelve a levantar, se yergue y se pone las manos en la cabeza, en la frente y en el cuello. A continuación adelanta el breve trecho que acaba de medir con su cuerpo y se vuelve a acostar en el suelo. Miles, miles de veces repite el procedimiento el peregrino hasta darle la vuelta a la montaña. En las manos y las rodillas lleva fijadas placas de madera que lo protegen de las piedras del suelo. Rodear el Kailashs se considera un recorrido simbólico del camino que va de la vida a la muerte y más allá, a través del estado intermedio, el "Bardo", hasta la reencarnación. Cada inclinación al suelo limpia el espíritu y permite reunir méritos en la vía hacia la iluminación.
Esta tierra de nieve está imbuida de una profunda religiosidad que sigue caracterizando la vida de los tibetanos hasta hoy. Y esto sigue siendo así incluso tras décadas de dominio forastero, durante el cual los chinos han intentado todo lo posible para extinguir la religión y el arte tibetanos. El 9 de septiembre de 1951 entraron 3 000 soldados chinos agitando banderas en la capital tibetana, Lhasa. Las peticiones de ayuda de los tibetanos a las Naciones Unidas no encontraron eco. Al principio los chinos no intervenían mucho en el día a día de los tibetanos, pero cada vez fueron estacionando más y más tropas. Finalmente fundaron "comunas populares" en las que los tibetanos estaban obligados a trabajar siete días a la semana. Al mismo tiempo los ocupantes colectivizaron la propiedad y el ganado de los tibe-

Tenzin Rintschen si prostra sul sentiero sassoso, si protende lentamente, si rialza, si raddrizza, congiunge le mani sulla testa, in fronte e sul collo. Avanza i pochi passi che ha appena misurato con il suo corpo, poi di nuovo a terra. Migliaia di volte su e giù, così il pellegrino fa il giro intorno al sacro monte. Tavolette di legno legate attorno alle ginocchia e alle mani lo proteggono dal fondo sassoso. Il periplo del Kailash è considerato un saggiare simbolico della strada che dalla vita porta nella morte per proseguire poi, attraverso lo stadio intermedio, il Bardo, in una nuova nascita. Ogni prostrazione purifica lo spirito e porta meriti sulla via dell'illuminazione.
Una religiosità profonda attraversa il Paese delle Nevi, pervade ancora oggi l'anima tibetana anche dopo decenni di dominio straniero, in cui i cinesi hanno fatto di tutto per annientare la religione e l'arte locali. Il 9 settembre 1951 3000 soldati cinesi entrarono nella capitale tibetana Lhasa brandendo le armi. Le grida di aiuto dei tibetani alle Nazioni Unite risuonarono invano. All'inizio gli occupanti si intromisero poco nella vita quotidiana dei tibetani, ma gli effettivi continuarono a crescere. Ad un certo punto allestirono comuni popolari dove costrinsero i tibetani al lavoro forzato sette giorni su sette. Allo stesso tempo gli occupanti collettivizzarono proprietà e bestiame dei tibetani. La risposta ad ogni forma di resistenza fu la distruzione di monasteri, esecuzioni, stupri, torture o deportazioni. Nel febbraio del 1959 il giovane Dalai Lama sostenne i suoi esami spirituali in vari monasteri. Il 10 marzo 1959 a Lhasa si scatenò un'insurrezione popolare contro gli occupanti. Dopo aver interrogato l'oracolo di stato e su pressione

Lama seine geistlichen Prüfungen in verschiedenen Klöstern ab. Am 10. März 1959 kam es in Lhasa zum Volksaufstand gegen die Besatzer. Nach Befragung des Staatsorakels und auf Drängen der Tibeter entschloss sich der damals 15-jährige Dalai Lama zur Flucht nach Indien. Die Gefahr, dass er von den Chinesen entführt oder ermordet worden wäre, war zu groß. Als Soldat verkleidet und durch Widerstandskämpfer geschützt, glückte ihm der wochenlange Ritt über die Himalajapässe. Lha Gyal lo. Seither setzt er sich unermüdlich und weltweit für seine Tibeter und Tibet ein.
In einem Gebet des Dalai Lama heißt es:
„So lange das Weltall besteht,
So lange Lebendiges lebt,
So lange möchte auch ich bestehen,
Um das Elend der Welt zu vertreiben.“
Während seiner Flucht tobten in Lhasa unterdessen erbitterte Kämpfe, die in einem Blutbad endeten. Die tibetische Regierung wurde abgesetzt, eine chinesische Militärdiktatur mit 140 000 Soldaten übernahm die Macht. In Tibet begann die systematische Zerstörung und Ausbeutung der Bevölkerung. 1,2 Millionen Tibeter, also fast jeder fünfte, starben in Arbeitslagern, bei Massakern oder verhungerten. Kombiniert mit dem gleichzeitig gezielten Zuzug von Chinesen wurden sie zur Minderheit im eigenen Land. Den rund fünf bis sechs Millionen Tibetern stehen an die zehn Millionen Chinesen gegenüber, die, gelockt durch Steuererleichterungen, Existenzgründungsprogramme oder als Soldaten ins Schneeland übersiedelten.
Die Zerstörung tibetischen Lebens erfasst auch Land und Kultur. In Beruf und Schule muss heute chinesisch gespro-

monasteries. On 10th March 1959, a popular uprising against the occupiers occurred in Lhasa. After consulting the state oracle, and at the urging of his people, the 15-year old Dalai Lama decided to take refuge in India. The danger that he might be abducted or assassinated by the Chinese was too great. Disguised as a soldier and protected by resistance fighters, he successfully made the week-long ride over the Himalayan passes. Lha Gyal lo. Since then, he has been tirelessly putting the case of his Tibetans and Tibet throughout the world. The words of a prayer of the Dalai Lama run:
“As long as the universe exists,
As long as living things breathe,
So long may I too exist,
To banish the misery of the world.”
During his flight, bitter fighting broke out in Lhasa, ending in a bloodbath. The Tibetan government was deposed, and a Chinese military dictatorship backed by 140,000 soldiers assumed power. In Tibet, the systematic destruction and exploitation of the population began. 1.2 million Tibetans, almost 20% of the total population, died in labour camps, in massacres or of starvation. Combined with the simultaneous and deliberate influx of Chinese, they became a minority in their own country. The five to six million Tibetans are now outnumbered by around 10 million Chinese, who have immigrated into the land of snow attracted by tax concessions, business start-up programmes or as soldiers.
The destruction of the Tibetan way of life extends to both the country and culture. Chinese is now the compulsory

destruction de monastères, des exécutions, des viols, des tortures ou la déportation. En février 1959, le jeune dalaï-lama passe avec succès ses divers examens spirituels dans divers monastères. Le 10 mars 1959, les habitants se révoltent à Lhassa contre les occupants. Après avoir interrogé l'oracle d'état et sur les instances des Tibétains, le dalaï-lama, alors âgé de 15 ans, décide de fuir en Inde, le risque d'être enlevé ou assassiné par les Chinois étant trop grand. Déguisé en soldat et protégé par des résistants, il parvient à traverser les cols de l'Himalaya après une chevauchée de plusieurs semaines. Lha Gyal lo. Depuis, il œuvre inlassablement pour son peuple et son pays à travers le monde entier. L'une des prières du dalaï-lama dit :

"Tant que durera l'espace
Et tant qu'il y aura des êtres vivants,
Puisse-je aussi contribuer
A dissiper la misère du monde."

Tandis qu'il fuit, des combats acharnés se déroulent à Lhassa et s'achèvent dans un bain de sang. Le gouvernement tibétain est déposé, une dictature chinoise, forte de 140 000 soldats, s'empare du pouvoir. Commencent alors au Tibet la destruction systématique et l'exploitation de la population. 1,2 millions de Tibétains, presque un cinquième de la population donc, périssent dans des camps de travail, sont massacrés ou meurent de faim. Ils deviennent, après l'arrivée organisée de nombreux Chinois, une minorité dans leur propre pays : cinq à six millions de Tibétains se trouvent en effet face à dix millions de Chinois qui, attirés par des baisses d'impôt, des programmes d'aides de départ ou au service de l'armée, s'établissent dans le Pays des Neiges.

tanos. Todos los intentos de resistencia fueron respondidos con destrucción de los monasterios, ejecuciones, violaciones, torturas o deportaciones. En febrero de 1959 el joven Dalai Lama terminó su ciclo de pruebas espirituales en diferentes monasterios. El 10 de marzo de 1959 se produjo en Lhasa un levantamiento popular contra los ocupantes. Tras consultar al oráculo del estado y respondiendo a las urgentes peticiones de los tibetanos, el Dalai Lama, que entonces tenía 15 años, se decidió a exiliarse en la India. El peligro de que hubiera sido secuestrado o asesinado por los chinos era demasiado grande. Disfrazado de soldado y protegido por miembros de la resistencia pudo culminar con éxito su huida de semanas de duración a través de los pasos del Himalaya. "Lha Gyal lo". Desde entonces se ha dedicado incansablemente en todo el mundo a la causa de sus tibetanos y del Tibet. En una oración del Dalai Lama se dice:

"En tanto siga existiendo el universo,
mientras aliente vida en los vivos,
quiero seguir existiendo,
para expulsar del mundo la maldad".

Durante su huida tuvieron lugar graves enfrentamientos en Lhasa, que acabaron en un baño de sangre. El gobierno tibetano fue depuesto y una dictadura militar china apoyada en 140 000 soldados asumió el poder. En Tibet se inició una fase de sistemática destrucción y de explotación de la población. 1,2 millones de tibetanos, es decir, uno de cada cinco, murió en los campos de trabajos forzados, fue asesinado en masacres o se murió de hambre. Todo ello en combinación con la organizada y sistemática colonización con chinos, fue convirtiendo a los tibetanos en una minoría

dei tibetani, l'allora quindicenne Dalai Lama fu messo in fuga verso l'India. Il pericolo che i cinesi lo rapissero o l'uccidessero era troppo grande. Travestito da soldato e protetto dai guerriglieri della resistenza, dopo settimane a cavallo riuscì a valicare i passi dell'Himalaya. Lha Gyal lo. Da allora si impegna instancabile in tutto il mondo per i suoi tibetani e il Tibet. In una preghiera del Dalai Lama si dice:

"Finché l'universo esiste,
finché ciò che ha vita vive,
fino a quel momento vorrei esserci anch'io,
per scacciare la miseria dal mondo."

Nel periodo della sua fuga a Lhasa imperversavano contemporeaneamente lotte accanite, che terminarono in un bagno di sangue. Il governo tibetano fu deposto, una dittatura militare cinese con 140 000 soldati prese il potere. In Tibet iniziò la distruzione sistematica e lo sfruttamento della popolazione. 1,2 milioni di tibetani, cioè quasi un quinto della popolazione, morì in campi di lavoro, in massacri o per fame. A ciò si aggiunse l'immigrazione mirata di cinesi e i tibetani diventarono la minoranza nel loro Paese. A cinque – sei milioni di tibetani fanno riscontro dieci milioni di cinesi, i quali, attirati da agevolazioni fiscali, programmi di aiuto all'insediamento o in veste di soldati, si stanziarono nel Paese delle Nevi. La distruzione della vita tibetana colpisce anche il Paese e la cultura. Sul lavoro e a scuola oggi si deve parlare in cinese. E così ci sono oggetti della vita moderna, come computer o telefono cellulare, per i quali non ci sono termini tibetani correnti. "La nostra lingua è diventata un pasticcio", dice triste una stu-

chen werden. Darum gibt es für Dinge des modernen Alltags wie Computer oder Mobiltelefon überhaupt keine gebräuchlichen tibetischen Wörter. „Unsere Sprache ist ein Mischmasch geworden", sagt eine Studentin aus Lhasa traurig. Wenn sie sich mit Freunden auf Tibetisch unterhalte, verwende sie in einem Satz oft drei oder vier chinesische Wörter. „Ich sehe unsere kulturelle Identität in Gefahr", fügt sie leise hinzu und blickt seufzend zum Potala hinauf.

Ragte nicht der strahlende Potala, der Winterpalast des Dalai Lama, stolz über der Stadt, wäre Lhasa heute ein hässliches, chinesisches Provinznest mit anonymen Betonbauten. Früher übte Lhasa eine magnetische Faszination auf Forscher und Abenteurer aus. Doch nur wenigen war es vergönnt, den Potala mit eigenen Augen zu sehen. Die eigentliche Residenz des Dalai Lama hat nichts von ihrer majestätischen Ausstrahlung verloren. Der Potala thront über Lhasa, dem heiligen Ort der Götter. Die Mauern des 13 Stockwerke hohen Palastes leuchten weiß, nur die eigentlichen Räumlichkeiten des Dalai Lama heben sich in Rot davon ab. Seine Räume werden immer noch so erhalten, wie er sie verlassen hat. Auf den goldenen Dächern des Palastes liegen die Tschorten, die Grabmäler der verstorbenen Dalai Lamas. Einmal nach Lhasa, einmal den Potala sehen ist für tibetische Pilger ebenso bedeutungsvoll, wie für Mohammedaner ein Besuch Mekkas.

Auch Nomaden im Hochland träumen davon. Seit Ewigkeiten waren die Tibeter Nomaden. In den grenzenlosen Weiten hat sich ihre Hirtenkultur nahezu unverfälscht erhalten. Wie Kleckse wirken die Zelte in der Landschaft,

language of business and education. As a result, there are simply no ordinary Tibetan words for modern day-to-day appliances such as computers or mobile telephones. "Our language has become a mishmash", says a female student from Lhasa sadly. When she converses with friends in Tibetan, she often uses three or four Chinese words in every sentence. "I fear that our cultural identity is in danger", she adds quietly, looking up with a sigh to the Potala Palace.

Were the ornate Potala Palace, the winter residence of the Dalai Lama, not to tower proudly over the city, Lhasa would today be an ugly, Chinese backwater of anonymous concrete buildings. In earlier times, Lhasa held a magnetic fascination for researchers and adventurers, though few were granted the privilege of seeing the Potala with their own eyes. The actual residence of the Dalai Lama has lost nothing of its majestic splendour. The Potala sits enthroned above Lhasa, the holy city of the gods. The walls of the 13-story Palace shine out in brilliant white, with only the apartments formerly used by the Dalai Lama standing out in red. The royal apartments have been maintained to the present day in the same condition as he left them. On the golden roofs of the palace lie the "stupa", the tombs of past Dalai Lamas. Making the journey to Lhasa at least once to see the Potala is just as important for Tibetan pilgrims as a visit to Mecca for Mohammedans.

The nomads of the highlands also dream of making such a trip. For centuries, the Tibetans were nomads. In the limitless expanses of the Himalayas, their pastoral culture has been preserved almost unchanged. Their tents, woven

La destruction de la vie tibétaine s'étend aussi au pays et à la culture. Au travail et à l'école, le Chinois est aujourd'hui obligatoire. C'est la raison pour laquelle il n'existe pas de mot tibétain pour désigner les objets de la vie quotidienne moderne comme par exemple un ordinateur ou un téléphone portable. „Notre langue est devenue un véritable embrouillamini", dit une étudiante de Lhassa avec tristesse. Lorsqu'elle parle avec des amis en tibétain, elle utilise souvent dans une seule phrase trois ou quatre mots chinois. „Notre identité culturelle est menacée", ajoute-t-elle doucement et lève les yeux en soupirant vers le Potala.

Si le resplendissant Potala, palais d'hiver du dalaï-lama, ne se dressait pas fièrement au-dessus de la ville, Lhassa ne serait aujourd'hui rien de plus qu'un affreux patelin de province chinois aux constructions en béton anonymes. Lhassa exerçait jadis une fascination magnétique sur les chercheurs et les aventuriers, mais rares sont ceux qui ont eu le privilège d'admirer de leurs propres yeux le Potala. La résidence proprement dite du dalaï-lama n'a rien perdu de son rayonnement majestueux et elle continue de trôner au-dessus de Lhassa, site sacré des Dieux. Les murs de cet édifice de treize étages abritent le Palais Blanc et le Palais Rouge où se trouvent les appartements du dalaï-lama qui sont conservés dans l'état dans lequel il les a quittés. Sur les toits de tuiles dorées du palais, des pagodes abritent les mausolées des défunts dalaï-lamas. Aller une fois dans sa vie à Lhassa, voir une fois dans sa vie au moins le Potala est aussi important pour un Tibétain qu'un pèlerinage à la Mecque pour un musulman.

en su propio país. Actualmente hay de cinco a seis millones de tibetanos frente a unos diez millones de chinos, que atraídos por incentivos fiscales, programas de promoción económica o como soldados fueron colonizando el país de las nieves.

La destrucción de la vida tibetana también ha afectado al país y su cultura. Tanto en la vida profesional como en la escuela se debe hablar hoy chino. Por ese motivo no hay palabras tibetanas utilizables para las cosas modernas de uso cotidiano, como el teléfono móvil y el ordenador.

Si el Potala, el palacio de invierno del Dalai Lama, no descollara orgulloso sobre la ciudad, hoy Lhasa sería una fea ciudad provinciana china compuesta de impersonales edificios de hormigón. Antiguamente Lhasa ejercía una fascinación magnética sobre exploradores y aventureros. Pero muy pocos tuvieron el privilegio de contemplar el Potala con sus propios ojos. La auténtica residencia del Dalai Lama no ha perdido nada de su majestuosa aura. El Potala domina Lhasa, el santuario sagrado de los dioses. Los muros del palacio de 13 plantas refulgen de blancura. Sólo los aposentos del Dalai Lama se destacan por su color rojo. Sus habitaciones se conservan todavía como él las abandonó. Sobre los dorados tejados del palacio se encuentran los "Tschorten", las tumbas de los pasados Dalai Lamas. Peregrinar una vez a Lhasa, poder ver una vez el Potala, es para los peregrinos tibetanos igual de importante que para los mahometanos una peregrinación a la Meca.

También los nómadas del altiplano sueñan con visitar Lhasa. Durante una gran parte de su historia los tibetanos fueron nómadas. En las llanuras sin límites su cultura pastoril

dentessa di Lhasa. Quando chiacchiera in tibetano con gli amici, spesso usa in una frase tre o quattro parole cinesi. "La nostra identità culturale è in pericolo", aggiunge sottovoce e sospira guardando il Potala.

Se il raggiante Potala, il palazzo invernale del Dalai Lama, non si ergesse orgoglioso sopra la città, Lhasa sarebbe un'orrenda cittadina di provincia cinese con anonime costruzioni di cemento.

Una volta Lhasa esercitava un fascino magnetico su ricercatori e avventurieri. Però a pochi era concesso di vedere il Potala con i propri occhi. La residenza effettiva del Dalai Lama non ha perso nulla della sua irradiazione maestosa. Il Potala troneggia su Lhasa, il luogo sacro degli dei. Le mura del palazzo alto 13 piani brillano di luce bianca, risalta solo il rosso dei locali dove risiede il Dalai Lama. Sui tetti d'oro del palazzo sono situati gli stupa, le tombe dei Dalai Lama precedenti. Essere stati una volta a Lhasa, aver visto una volta il Potala, per i pellegrini tibetani riveste un'importanza enorme, come una visita alla Mecca per i musulmani.

È un sogno anche per i nomadi degli altipiani. Da tempi immemorabili i tibetani sono nomadi. Nelle distese sterminate la loro cultura pastorizia si è conservata quasi genuina. Le loro tende tessute di lana di yak e sostenute da alti pali esterni punteggiano il paesaggio come macchioline. Lo yak, una specie di manzo, è il loro animale più importante: perfettamente adattato al clima e alle altitudini elevate, serve come animale da sella e da soma e può trasportare fino a 150 chili. Il suo folto pelo viene tessuto, la pelle conciata, la carne essiccata. Persino gli escrementi

aus Yakhaaren gewebt sind sie mit hohen Außenpfosten verspannt. Der Yak, eine Art Rind, ist ihr wichtigstes Tier, denn es ist perfekt an das Klima und die gewaltigen Höhen angepasst und dient als Reit- und Lasttier, das bis zu 150 Kilo schleppen kann. Seine dichten Haare werden versponnen, die Häute gegerbt, das Fleisch getrocknet. Sogar sein Kot wird als Brennmaterial in den baumlosen Gegenden gesammelt. Die fettreiche Milch der Yakkühe verarbeiten die Nomaden zu Butter. Butter wiederum ist die Hauptzutat für das Nationalgetränk auf dem Dach der Welt, den Buttertee. Eine eher bouillonartige Brühe, bestehend aus Tee, Salz und Butter, die Energielieferant ist und hilft, auch bei extremer Kälte die Körpertemperatur aufrechtzuhalten. Für die meisten Nicht-Tibeter schmeckt Buttertee mehr als gewöhnungsbedürftig. Für Tibeter verheißt er zusammen mit Tsampa ein köstliches Essen. Tsampa, das Grundnahrungsmittel, ist schnell und einfach zubereitet. Es ist nichts weiter als geröstetes Gerstenmehl, das die Einheimischen in eine Schüssel füllen, mit Buttertee übergießen, mit den Fingern durchmischen, bis es zu Teig geworden ist. Egal ob Nomade, Schafhändler oder Mönch, Tsampa gehört für jeden Tibeter auf den Tisch.

Mönchen und Klöstern kommen im Schneeland eine besondere Bedeutung zu. In den Klöstern bündeln sich Wissen, Bildung, Kunst und, vor dem Einmarsch der Chinesen, auch weltliche Macht. Früher gab es tausende großer und kleiner Klöster. Für das Volk waren sie Stätten der Verehrung, für deren Unterhalt man sorgte und in die man mindestens einen Sohn als Mönch schickte. Heute sind die meisten zerstört, die Kunstschätze geplündert, Bücher

from yak hair and tensioned by tall external posts, look like splashes of colour amongst the landscape. The yak, a species of cattle, is the most important type of livestock; it is perfectly adapted to the climate and the great height, and is used both for riding and as a beast of burden, which can carry up to 150 kg. Its thick hair is spun into filament, the hides tanned and the meat dried. Even its dung is collected for fuel in barren, treeless regions. Cow yaks produce milk rich in fat, which the nomads churn to make butter, which forms the main ingredient of the national drink here at the roof of the world, butter tea – actually a type of broth made with tea, salt and butter, which is a great energy supplier, and also helps to maintain the body temperature in very cold weather. For most non-Tibetans, butter tea takes some getting used to, although for Tibetans, it makes a delicious meal together with tsampa. Tsampa, the staple foodstuff, is easy and quick to prepare. It is no more than roasted barley flour, which the locals place in a bowl, add butter tea and knead with their fingers until it forms into a dough. Whether for nomads, sheepherders or monks, tsampa is an essential part of every Tibetan's diet.

Monks and monasteries are particularly revered in this land of snow. The monasteries were the seat of knowledge, education, art, and before the invasion by the Chinese, also temporal power. Formerly there were thousands of monasteries, large and small. For the people, they were places of veneration, which were maintained by the populace and to which every family usually sent at least one son as a monk. Today most have been destroyed, the art

Les nomades sur les hauts plateaux en rêvent également. Les Tibétains ont été des nomades de tout temps. Dans les immensités sans fin, ils ont su conserver leur culture pastorale. Leurs tentes, tissées avec des poils de yacks et tendues au moyen de hauts piquets, font des tâches dans le paysage. Le yack, voisin du bœuf, est un animal primordial pour eux car il est parfaitement adapté au climat et aux altitudes vertigineuses tout en étant un animal de selle et de bât pouvant porter ou tirer jusqu'à 150 kilos. On tisse sa toison touffue, on tanne sa peau, on sèche sa viande et on utilise même ses excréments en guise de combustible dans les régions non boisées. Les femelles donnent un lait très riche en graisses à partir duquel les nomades fabriquent du beurre. Celui-ci à son tour est le principal ingrédient de la boisson nationale sur le Toit du Monde, le thé au beurre. Il s'agit plutôt d'une sorte de bouillon à base de thé, de sel et de beurre très énergétique qui aide également, lorsqu'il fait très froid, à maintenir la température du corps. La plupart des étrangers ont du mal à ingurgiter cette boisson, mais pour les Tibétains en revanche, elle constitue avec le zamba un délicieux repas. Le zamba, aliment de base, est facile et rapide à préparer. Ce n'est que de la farine d'orge grillée dont les autochtones remplissent un bol avant de verser dessus du thé au beurre, puis de mélanger le tout avec les doigts jusqu'à obtenir une pâte. Qu'il soit nomade, marchand de brebis ou moine, impossible pour un Tibétain d'imaginer un repas sans zamba.

Les moines et les monastères occupent une place particulière au Pays des Neiges. Les monastères abritent le savoir, la culture, l'art et même, avant l'arrivée des Chinois, le pouvoir temporel. Les monastères, petits et grands, se

ha podido conservarse casi pura. Las tiendas, que están tejidas con pelo de yak y se estiran sobre altas estacas de sujeción, parecen manchas en el paisaje. El yak, un tipo de bóvido, es su animal doméstico más importante, ya que está perfectamente adaptado al clima y a las enormes alturas. El yak se utiliza como montura y animal de carga que puede transportar hasta 150 kilos. Su tupido pelo se utiliza para tejer, sus pieles se curten y la carne se seca. Incluso sus excrementos se utilizan como combustible en las llanuras desprovistas de árboles. Las hembras del yak producen una leche grasa que los nómadas utilizan para hacer mantequilla. La mantequilla es el principal ingrediente de la bebida nacional del techo del mundo: el té de mantequilla. Se trata de una especie de caldo compuesto de té, sal y mantequilla que no sólo proporciona mucha energía, sino que también ayuda a mantener constante la temperatura del cuerpo incluso con fríos extremos. Para la mayoría de los forasteros el té de mantequilla tiene un sabor al que es difícil de acostumbrarse. Sin embargo para los tibetanos supone junto al "tsampa" una buena comida. El "tsampa", el alimento básico, se puede preparar con rapidez y facilidad. No es otra cosa que harina tostada de cebada que los tibetanos echan en un cuenco, la riegan con té de mantequilla y lo mezclan todo con los dedos hasta que han formado una masa. Para todos los tibetanos, ya sean nómadas, vendedores de ovejas o monjes, el "tsampa" es una parte imprescindible de la comida.

Los monjes y los monasterios tienen una importancia especial en la tierra de las nieves. En los monasterios se concentran la sabiduría, la educación, el arte y, hasta la ocupación china, también el poder profano. Antiguamente había

vengono raccolti per essere usati come combustibile nelle zone dove non ci sono alberi. Le femmine yak forniscono un latte ricco di grassi, che i nomadi lavorano in burro. A sua volta il burro è l'ingrediente principale per la bevanda nazionale sul Tetto del Mondo, il tè al burro, una specie di brodo con tè, sale e burro, fornitore di energie che aiuta a mantenere la temperatura del corpo anche in condizioni di freddo rigido. Per la maggior parte dei non-tibetani il tè al burro necessita di una certa assuefazione. Per i tibetani è insieme alla tsampa un pasto squisito. La preparazione della tsampa, l'alimento base, è semplice e rapida. Non è nient'altro che farina di orzo tostata che i locali versano in una terrina, cospargono di tè al burro e impastano con le dita. La tsampa è un piatto che viene servito sulla tavola di ogni tibetano, nomadi, commercianti di pecore o monaci che siano.

I monaci e i monasteri rivestono un ruolo particolare nel Paese delle Nevi. I monasteri sono fulcri di sapere, istruzione, arte e, fino all'avanzata cinese, erano anche centri di potere temporale. Una volta c'erano migliaia di monasteri grandi e piccoli. Per la popolazione erano luoghi di venerazione, si provvedeva al loro mantenimento e ogni famiglia vi mandava almeno un figlio. Oggi la maggior parte di essi è distrutta, le opere d'arte saccheggiate, libri e manoscritti bruciati, statue e oggetti rituali preziosi convertiti in valute. Un po' alla volta i tibetani ricostruiscono alcuni dei monasteri, come il monastero distrutto di Ganden, a simboleggiare la loro inflessibilità, la resistenza dello spirito. Solo i monasteri che possono servire da attrazioni turistiche ricevono sussidi statali per la ricostruzione.

und Handschriften verbrannt, wertvolle Statuen und Ritualgegenstände in Devisen umgesetzt. Die Tibeter bauen manche der Klöster, wie das zerstörte Ganden, allmählich wieder auf. Dies gilt als Symbol für ihre Unbeugsamkeit, für den Widerstand des Geistes. Nur die Klöster, die sich als touristische Sehenswürdigkeiten nutzen lassen, erhalten staatliche Zuschüsse für den Wiederaufbau.

Früher kamen die Novizen bereits mit sechs oder sieben Jahren ins Kloster und wurden einem Lehrer anvertraut, der auch die Elternrolle übernahm. Heute geht das fast nur noch außerhalb Tibets, in indischen oder nepalesischen Exilklöstern. Tibetische Eltern schicken ihre Kinder unter Lebensgefahr dorthin, um ihnen eine traditionelle Ausbildung zu ermöglichen. Zunächst lernen sie Lesen, Schreiben, Rechnen, Kalligrafie und widmen sich ausgiebig dem Auswendiglernen buddhistischer Texte, die die Grundlage der späteren Ausbildung sind. Oft werden auch weltliche Fächer wie Geografie oder Englisch unterrichtet. Die weitere Ausbildung hängt von den individuellen Talenten der jungen Mönche ab. Schulung in Rhetorik und die Kunst des Debattierens gehören ebenso dazu, wie das Studium der Mönchsregeln, die Unterweisung in Rituale und natürlich regelmäßige Meditation, mit dem Ziel, sich von Begierden zu befreien, die Ursache allen Leidens sind.

Leiden mussten viele tibetische Arbeiter für den Bau der Lhasa-Bahn, wie sie im Volksmund heißt. Die Qinghai-Tibet-Bahn, ihr eigentlicher Name, ist das bisher gewaltigste Eisenbahnprojekt dieses Jahrhunderts und umfasst 1956 Streckenkilometer, davon sind 960 auf mehr als 4 000

treasures plundered, books and manuscripts burnt and valuable statues and ritual objects converted into foreign currency. The Tibetans are gradually rebuilding some of them, such as the destroyed Ganden Monastery. This constitutes a symbol of their intractability, of the resistance of the spirit. Only the monasteries which can serve as tourist attractions receive state grants for reconstruction.

In earlier times, the novices entered the monastery at the age of six or seven, where they were placed under the charge of a teacher, who also took over the parental role. Today this tradition continues almost only outside Tibet, in "monasteries in exile" in India or Nepal. Tibetan parents send their children there, at the risk of their lives, in order to give them a traditional education. First they learn reading, writing, arithmetic and calligraphy, and devote themselves particularly to learning by heart the Buddhist texts which form the basis of their later education. Worldly subjects such as geography or English are also taught in many cases. The further education depends on the individual talents and abilities of the young monks. Training in rhetoric and the art of debate are also included, as well as the study of the monks' code, instruction in rituals and of course regular meditation, with the aim of becoming free of earthly desires, the cause of all suffering.

Suffering was the lot of many Tibetan workers for the construction of the Lhasa railway, as it is popularly known. The Qinghai-Tibet railway, its official name, is the most ambitious railway project of the century so far, and extends 1,956 kilometres, 960 of which run at a height of over 4,000 metres, making it the highest-altitude railway line

comptaient autrefois par milliers. Lieux de culte pour le peuple, celui-ci veillait à son entretien et chaque famille y envoyait au moins un fils pour devenir moine. Aujourd'hui, la plupart de ces monastères ont été détruits, leurs trésors dérobés, les livres et manuscrits qui s'y trouvaient brûlés, les statues précieuses et objets ritualistes convertis en devises. Les Tibétains reconstruisent peu à peu certains monastères comme le Ganden qui avait été dévasté. Cela pour manifester symboliquement leur inflexibilité, la résistance de l'esprit. Seule la reconstruction des monastères considérés comme des attractions touristiques, est aujourd'hui subventionnée par l'Etat.

Autrefois, les novices entraient au monastère dès l'âge de six ou sept ans et étaient confiés à un professeur qui prenait la place des parents auprès de l'enfant. Aujourd'hui, cela n'est quasiment possible que hors du Tibet, dans les monastères d'exil en Inde ou au Népal. Les parents tibétains y envoient leurs enfants au péril de leur vie pour leur permettre de recevoir une éducation traditionnelle. Ils apprennent d'abord à lire, à écrire, à compter, mais aussi à calligraphier et consacrent une grande partie de leur temps à apprendre par cœur les textes bouddhistes qui sont la base de leur formation ultérieure. On leur enseigne aussi souvent des matières temporelles telles que la géographie ou l'anglais. La suite de leur éducation dépend des dons de chaque moine. Les novices suivent également un enseignement de rhétorique et apprennent à débattre tout en étudiant les règles monacales les rituels et naturellement la méditation régulière afin de se délivrer des désirs, cause de toute souffrance.

miles de pequeños y grandes monasterios. Para el pueblo se trataba de lugares de veneración que se conservaban de forma comunitaria y a los cuales se enviaba como mínimo un hijo para que se hiciera monje. Hoy la mayoría han sido destruidos, los tesoros artísticos saqueados, los libros y manuscritos quemados, valiosas estatuas y objetos de culto fueron vendidos por divisas. Actualmente los tibetanos van reconstruyendo poco a poco algunos monasterios como el destruido monasterio de Ganden. De esta forma asientan un símbolo de su supervivencia como pueblo, de la resistencia de su espíritu. Sólo los monasterios que se pueden usar como atracciones turísticas reciben subvenciones estatales para su reconstrucción.

Antiguamente los novicios ingresaban ya con seis o siete años en el monasterio y eran puestos bajo la responsabilidad de un maestro que también asumía las funciones de los padres. Hoy esto casi sólo es posible fuera de Tibet, en monasterios del exilio en la India o en Nepal. Los padres tibetanos envían allí a sus hijos, incluso a riesgo de sus vidas, para que reciban una educación tradicional. Primero aprenden a leer y a escribir, aritmética y caligrafía, se dedican al aprendizaje de memoria de textos budistas que forman la base de su posterior educación. A menudo también se imparte asignaturas profanas como geografía o inglés. La educación posterior depende de los talentos del joven monje. La formación retórica y el arte del debate son, al igual que las reglas de la vida monástica, la instrucción sobre los rituales y, naturalmente, la meditación regular, parte del programa avanzado. La meditación tiene el objetivo de liberarse de las ansias de este mundo, que son la causa de todos los males.

Una volta i novizi entravano già a sei o sette anni in monastero, dove venivano affidati ad un maestro il quale assumeva anche del ruolo dei genitori. Oggi questo è possibile quasi solo fuori dal Tibet, in monasteri in esilio in India o in Nepal. Rischiando la vita, i genitori tibetani vi mandano i figli per dare loro una formazione tradizionale. Là imparano prima a leggere, a scrivere, a far di conto, a cimentarsi con la calligrafia e poi si dedicano intensamente ad imparare a memoria testi buddisti, la base della loro formazione successiva. Spesso si insegnano anche materie secolari, come geografia o inglese. Il seguito dipende dai talenti individuali dei giovani monaci. Fanno parimenti parte dell'istruzione la retorica e l'arte del dibattere, lo studio delle regole dei monaci, l'iniziazione ai rituali e ovviamente meditazione regolare con l'obiettivo di liberare dalle brame, che sono all'origine di tutte le sofferenze.

Purtroppo molti lavoratori tibetani dovettero lavorare per la costruzione della ferrovia di Lhasa, come viene comunemente chiamata. La linea ferroviaria Qinghai-Tibet, questo il suo vero nome, è sinora il progetto ferroviario più imponente di questo secolo e comprende un percorso di 1956 chilometri, di cui 960 su oltre 4 000 metri di altitudine. È considerata la ferrovia più in quota del mondo. Ora è possibile percorrere i 4 000 chilometri da Pechino a Lhasa in 48 ore. Un quarto del percorso è stato costruito sul permafrost, che in estate sgela per breve tempo potendo provocare l'abbassamento del tracciato. Per evitare che il terreno si sgeli e il tracciato quindi si abbassi, i lavoratori hanno inserito nel sottosuolo barre di raffreddamento piene di ammoniaca. Se questo ha avuto successo? Già un

Meter Höhe. Damit gilt sie als höchstgelegene Bahnstrecke der Welt. Nun ist es möglich, in 48 Stunden die rund 4 000 Kilometer von Peking nach Lhasa zurückzulegen. Ein Viertel der Strecke ist auf Permafrostboden gebaut, der im Sommer kurz auftaut. Das könnte zum Absinken der Trasse führen. Um zu verhindern, dass der Boden auftaut und sich die Trasse dadurch senkt, trieben die Arbeiter mit Ammoniak gefüllte Kühlstäbe in den Boden. Ob dies so erfolgreich war? Schon einen Monat nach Eröffnung der Strecke erklärte das Eisenbahnministerium, dass sich erste Risse gebildet haben, weil der Boden unter der Bahnlinie leicht gesunken sei. Dennoch: Mit der Lhasa-Bahn lassen sich Bodenschätze leichter abtransportieren, aber auch Öl, Kohle oder Baustoffe schneller nach Tibet bringen. Und für Touristen ist es eine atemberaubende und atemraubende Fahrt durch Wüstenlandstriche, vorbei an Nomaden und ihren grasenden Yakherden. Schier endlose Weite. Am Horizont die weißen Gipfel des Himalaja und darüber leuchtet der tiefblaue Himmel. Blau, Weiß, Grau und Grün, die Farben für das Dach der Welt.

in the world. It is now possible to cover the approx. 4,000 kilometres from Peking to Lhasa in 48 hours. A quarter of the line is built on permafrost ground, which only thaws briefly during the summer. This could lead to settlement of the line. In order to prevent the ground thawing and the line subsiding, the workers drove cooling piles filled with ammonia into the ground. Did this prove a success? Only one month after the opening of the line, the Railway Ministry announced that the first cracks had already formed, because the ground under the line had subsided slightly. Nevertheless: thanks to the Lhasa railway, mineral resources can be transported away more easily, and oil, coal and construction materials transported to Tibet more quickly. And for tourists, it makes a breathtaking journey through a wilderness landscape, past nomads and their grazing yak herds. An unending vastness, with the snow-capped peaks of the Himalayas on the horizon, surmounted by the deep azure blue of the sky. Blue, white, grey and green, the colours of the roof of the world.

De nombreux ouvriers Tibétains ont souffert pour construire la ligne Pékin-Lhassa comme on l'appelle là-bas. La liaison ferroviaire Qinghai-Tibet, de son vrai nom, est le projet ferroviaire le plus ambitieux de ce siècle et s'étire sur 1 956 kilomètres de voie dont 960 à plus de 4 000 m d'altitude. Il s'agit donc de la ligne ferroviaire la plus haute du monde grâce à laquelle il est possible, aujourd'hui, de parcourir en 48 heures les 4 000 kilomètres environ qui séparent Pékin de Lhassa. Un quart de la distance passe par un sol gelé toute l'année qui ne dégèle que brièvement en été, cela pouvant entraîner un affaissement de la voie. Pour éviter le dégel du sol et palier au risque d'affaissement, les ouvriers ont fait des trous dans le sol et enfoncé des tubes remplis d'ammoniaque solide. Cette solution s'est-elle révélée efficace ? Un mois à peine après l'inauguration de la ligne, le ministère des chemins de fer a annoncé que les premières fissures étaient déjà apparues suite au léger affaissement du sol sous la voie. Pourtant, grâce à cette liaison, il est plus facile d'expédier les richesses naturelles du sol, mais aussi d'amener plus rapidement au Tibet le pétrole, le charbon ou les matériaux de construction. Et pour les touristes, ce voyage à travers des contrées désertiques, sous le regard parfois de nomades avec leurs troupeaux de yacks en train de brouter, est une aventure époustouflante. Une immensité sans fin avec, à l'horizon, les sommets blancs de l'Himalaya et au-dessus le bleu profond resplendissant du ciel. Bleu, blanc, gris et vert, les couleurs du Toit du Monde.

Muchos trabajadores tibetanos tuvieron que padecer mucho en los trabajos de construcción del ferrocarril a Lhasa, que es como el pueblo llama al ferrocarril Qinghai-Tibet. Se trata del más ambicioso proyecto de construcción de una línea ferroviaria de este siglo y abarca un trecho de 1956 kilómetros, de los cuales 960 están a más de 4 000 metros de altura. Por ello se considera la línea de ferrocarril más elevada del mundo. De esta forma es posible recorrer en 48 horas los alrededor de 4 000 kilómetros de distancia entre Pekín y Lhasa. Una cuarta parte de la línea ferroviaria fue construida sobre gelisuelo que sólo queda libre de hielo brevemente durante el verano. Esto podría dar lugar a un hundimiento de las vías. Para evitar que el suelo se derrita y el trazado ferroviario se hunda, los trabajadores introdujeron en el gelisuelo barras de refrigeración rellenas de amoniaco. ¿Tuvo éxito el procedimiento? Tan sólo un mes después de la inauguración de la línea, el Ministerio de Ferrocarriles declaró que se habían formado las primeras grietas porque el suelo bajo la línea férrea se había hundido ligeramente. Y a pesar de todo, con el ferrocarril a Lhasa resulta más fácil llevarse las riquezas minerales pero también transportar con mayor rapidez petróleo, carbón o materiales de construcción a Tibet. Y el viaje en ferrocarril se ha convertido para los turistas en una impresionante experiencia que roba el aliento. La línea pasa por paisajes de desierto, junto a los rebaños de yaks de los nómadas a través de estepas que parecen no tener límites. En el horizonte se adivinan las blancas cimas del Himalaya y más allá resplandece el azul profundo del cielo. Azul, blanco, gris y verde, los colores del techo del mundo.

mese dopo l'inaugurazione del tracciato il ministro delle ferrovie ha dichiarato che si erano formate le prime crepe perché il terreno sotto la linea ferroviaria si era leggermente abbassato. Se con la ferrovia di Lhasa si possono trasportare più facilmente le ricchezze del sottosuolo si possono comunque far arrivare più velocemente in Tibet il petrolio, il carbone o i materiali da costruzione. E per i turisti percorrere i territori deserti costeggiando i campi dei nomadi e le loro mandrie di yak al pascolo è un'emozione fortissima e una suggestione unica. Una distesa sterminata. All'orizzonte le cime bianche dell'Himalaya si stagliano nell'azzurro intenso del cielo. Azzurro, bianco, grigio e verde, i colori del Tetto del Mondo.

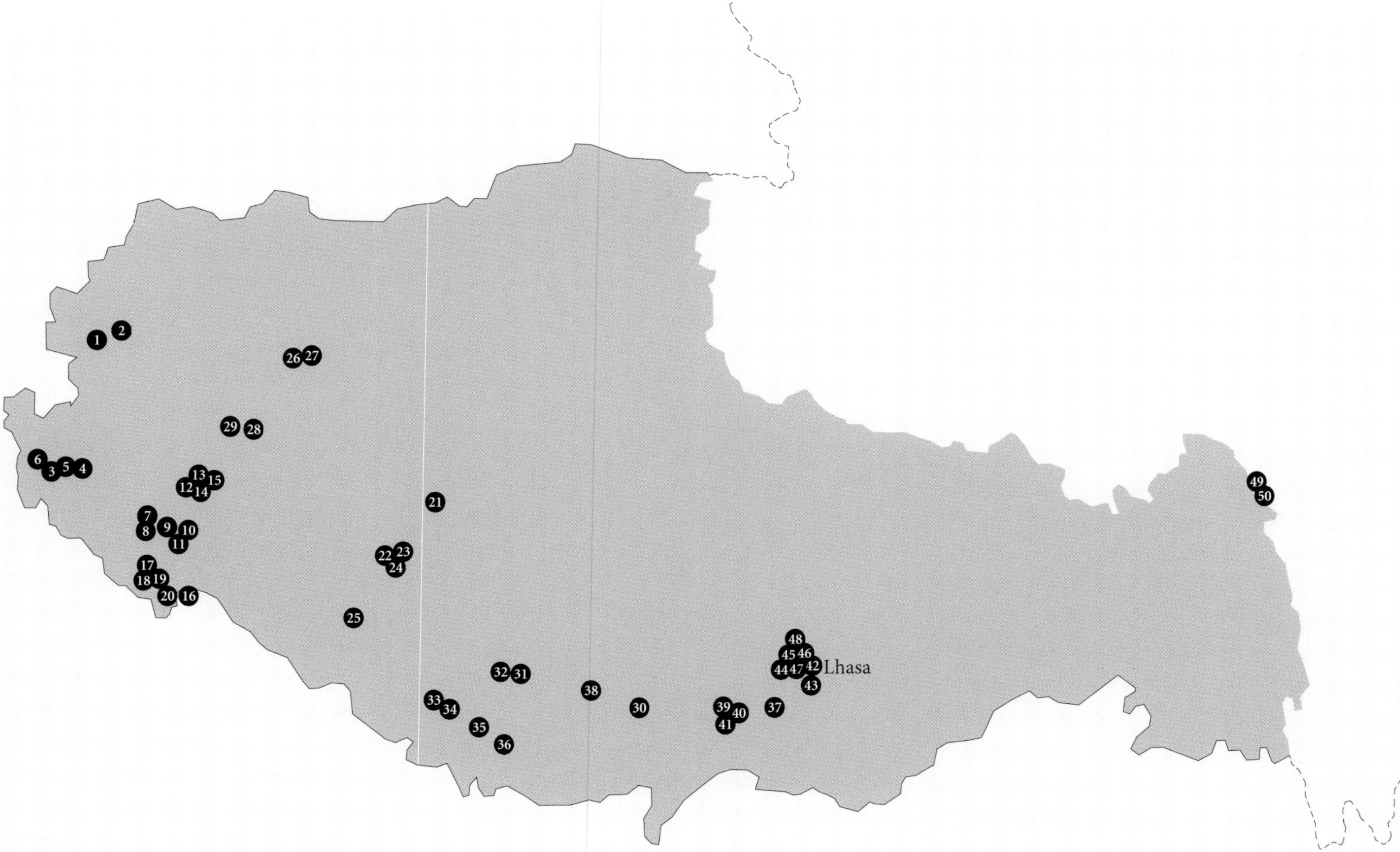
1
2
26
27
29
28
6
3
5
4
13
15
12
14
21
7
9
10
8
11
22
23
24
17
18
19
20
16
25
49
50
48
45
46
44
47
42
Lhasa
43
32
31
38
33
34
30
39
40
37
41
35
36

1 Yak herd on the southern limits of the Aksai Chin

3 The Sutlej Valley between Tholing and Tsaparang

4 The great chorten at Tholing

5 Remains of the temples at Tholing

6 Ruins at Tsaparang

7 Mount Kailash, seen from the north

8 Mount Kailash, seen from the south

9 Barga, in the background Gurla Mandhata

10 Lake Manasarovar

11 Chiu Gompa on the shores of Lake Manasorvar

12 Nomads shearing wool at Lungdep

13 Lungdep

14 Rungmagem

15 Nomad camp in Rungmagem

16 Trade center on the upper reaches of the Karnali

17 Nepali Mandi, a market of Nepali traders on the outskirts of Purang

18 Near Purang

19 Near Purang

21 Countryside near Tsochen

22 Transhimalaya, near the source of Raga-Tsangpo

23 Transhimalaya

24 A lake at 5 300 m in the Transhimalaya

25 Tsangpo ferry

26 Nomad tent on the Chang Tang

27 Milking goats on the Chang Tang

28 Nomad tent between Gertse and Tsaga

29 Salt lake near Tsaga

30 Road to West Tibet south of Shigatse

31 Countryside between Ngamring and Sangsang in the Raga-Tsangpo Valley

32 Nomads near Sangsang

33 On the northern shore of Paikü Tso

34 A group of Tewa nomads

35 Village Gurtso on the Kathmandu–Lhasa road

36 Tingri, a station on the Kathmandu–Lhasa road

37 Lake Yamdrok

38 Sakya, the southern monastery

39 View of Gyantse

40 View of Gyantse from the top of the Dzong

41 Remains of the monastic city Gyantse

42 Potala in Lhasa

43 Ganden, one of the state monasteries before 1959

44 Nechung, formerly the seat of the state oracle

45 Main entrance to the Jokhang

47 On the roof of the Jokhang

48 View across the Lhasa Valley from Sera

49 Countryside at Chola-la

50 Village near Derge

JAROSLAV PONCAR wurde 1945 in Prag geboren. Heute lebt er in Köln, wo er seit 1973 als Professor im Fachbereich Photoingenieurwesen und Medientechnik tätig ist. Seine zahlreichen photographisch motivierten Reisen führten ihn meistens in den Himalaya und nach Tibet, nach Zentralasien, Indien und nach Kambodscha. Seit 1976 entwickelte er eine besondere Vorliebe für die Panoramaphotographie. Als erster Europäer durchquerte er 1985 Tibet in seiner gesamten Ost-West-Ausdehnung. Im Jahr darauf schloss er sich für längere Zeit tibetischen Nomaden an. Als Mitglied des German Apsara Conservation Project ist er derzeit im Rahmen des UNESCO-Programms zur Erhaltung von Angkor für die umfassendste Photodokumentation über Angkor Wat in Kambodscha verantwortlich.

IRIS LEMANCZYK wurde 1964 in Kirchheim/Teck bei Stuttgart geboren. Nach dem Studium der Germanistik und Geographie lockte immer wieder die Ferne. Sie reiste um die Welt, schnupperte eine Zeit lang Zirkusluft, lebte in Namibia und besuchte für ein paar Monate Australien und Neuseeland. Dazwischen arbeitete sie bei der „Südwest Presse" in Ulm. Seit 1997 ist sie freiberuflich tätig, schreibt Kinder- und Jugendbücher sowie Sachbücher, verfasst Reiseberichte und ist als Dozentin für Kreatives Schreiben tätig.

JAROSLAV PONCAR was born in Prague in 1945. He now lives in Cologne, where he has since 1973 been Professor for Photo Engineering and Media Technology at the University of the Applied Sciences. His countless, photographically motivated travels have usually taken him to the Himalayas and Tibet, to Central Asia, India and Cambodia. Since 1976 he has developed an especial preference for panorama photography. In 1985, he was the first European to cross Tibet from East to West. The following year he spent many months with Tibetan nomads. As a member of the German Apsara Conservation Project he is currently in charge of the truly comprehensive photographic documentation of Angkor Wat in Cambodia as part of the UNESCO program for the preservation of Angkor.

IRIS LEMANCZYK was born in 1964 in Kirchheim/Teck near Stuttgart. After studying German and geography, she gave way to the call of far-distant places. She travelled around the world, experienced the circus life for a time, lived in Namibia and spent several months in Australia and New Zealand. In between, she also learnt something more conventional: newspaper editing with the "Südwest Presse" in Ulm. Since 1997 she has worked as a freelancer, writing children's books and non-fiction and compiling travel reports, and also works as a lecturer on creative writing.

JAROSLAV PONCAR est né à Prague en 1945 mais il vit aujourd'hui à Cologne où il est depuis 1973 professeur de technique de la photographie et des médias. Les nombreux voyages qu'il a réalisés pour faire des photos l'ont entraîné le plus souvent vers l'Himalaya et le Tibet, l'Asie Centrale, l'Inde et le Cambodge. Depuis 1976, il s'intéresse tout particulièrement à la photographie panoramique. Il a été le premier Européen à traverser le Tibet d'est en ouest en 1985. L'année suivante, il se joint pendant une longue période à des nomades tibétains. Membre de l'organisation «German Apsara Conservation Project“, il est actuellement chargé de réaliser une vaste documentation photo pour la préservation du site d'Angkor Wat au Cambodge dans le cadre du programme de l'UNESCO.

IRIS LEMANCZYK est née en 1964 à Kirchheim/Teck près de Stuttgart. Après des études de philologie allemande et de géographie, elle effectue régulièrement des voyages lointains. Elle voyage à travers le monde, séjourne pendant quelque temps dans un cirque, vit en Namibie et passe plusieurs mois en Australie et en Nouvelle-Zélande. Entre toutes ces occupations, elle trouve néanmoins le temps d'apprendre un métier sérieux : rédactrice journalistique au quotidien allemand « Südwest Presse » à Ulm. Depuis 1997, elle travaille comme rédactrice indépendante, écrit des livres destinés à l'enfance et à la jeunesse ainsi que des livres d'essai. Elle rédige également des comptes rendus de voyage et dispense des cours de création littéraire.

JAROSLAV PONCAR nació en 1945 en Praga. Actualmente vive en Colonia, donde ejerce desde 1973 como profesor de Ingeniería de la Fotografía y Tecnología de los Medios de Comunicación. Sus numerosos viajes fotográficos le han llevado sobre todo al Himalaya y al Tibet, a Asia Central, a la India y a Camboya. Desde 1976 ha desarrollado una especial predilección por la fotografía panorámica. En 1985 se convirtió en el primer europeo que atravesó completamente el Tibet de este a oeste. El año siguiente se unió durante un prolongado período de tiempo a los nómadas tibetanos. Actualmente Jaroslav Poncar ejerce en su calidad de miembro de la asociación alemana "German Apsara Conservation Project" y en el marco de su colaboración con el programa de conservación de la UNESCO para salvar Angkor, la responsabilidad sobre la confección de la más extensa documentación fotográfica realizada hasta el momento sobre Angkor Wat en Camboya.

IRIS LEMANCZYK nació en 1964 en el pueblo de Kirchheim/Teck junto a Stuttgart. Tras terminar su carrera de Filología Germánica y Geografía se dejó atraer cada vez más por el encanto de los destinos exóticos: viajó por el mundo, experimentó durante algún tiempo la vida en un circo, residió en Namibia y pasó algunos meses en Australia y Nueva Zelanda. Y entre todas esas ocupaciones todavía encontró tiempo para aprender un oficio serio: redactora de periódicos en la editorial alemana "Südwest Presse" de Ulm. Desde 1997 trabaja como redactora libre y escribe diversos libros: desde literatura infantil y juvenil a libros de texto. Además confecciona relatos de viaje e imparte seminarios de creación literaria.

JAROSLAV PONCAR è nato nel 1945 a Praga. Oggi vive a Colonia, dove lavora dal 1973 come professore alla facoltà di ingegneria fotografica e tecniche mediali. I suoi numerosi viaggi all'insegna della fotografia lo hanno portato il più delle volte nell'Himalaya e nel Tibet, nell'Asia centrale, in India e in Cambogia. Dal 1976 iniziò ad emergere la sua particolare passione per la fotografia panoramica. Nel 1985 egli fu il primo europeo ad attraversare interamente il Tibet dall'estremità orientale a quella occidentale. L'anno successivo si trattenne per un periodo piuttosto lungo presso i nomadi tibetani. Quale membro del German Apsara Conservation Project, Jaroslav Poncar è attualmente responsabile, nell'ambito del programma dell'UNESCO per la salvaguardia del sito archeologico di Angkor, del più ampio documentario fotografico sul tempio Angkor Wat in Cambogia.

IRIS LEMANCZYK è nata nel 1964 a Kirchheim/Teck vicino a Stoccarda. Dopo la laurea in Lingua e Letteratura Tedesca e in Geografia ha seguito la sua passione per i viaggi in paesi lontani. È stata in tutto il mondo, per un certo periodo ha respirato l'aria del circo, ha vissuto in Namibia e per qualche mese ha abitato in Australia e Nuova Zelanda. Tra un viaggio e l'altro si è dedicata alla più razionale attività di redattrice presso la Südwest Presse di Ulm. Dal 1997 lavora come libera professionista, scrive libri per bambini e ragazzi e testi di saggistica, redige reportage di viaggi ed insegna scrittura creativa.

ISBN: 978-3-89823-349-1

Concept: Bernhard Wipfler, Sebastian Wipfler, Marcus Bela Schmitt
Design: EDITION PANORAMA | Diana May and Designgruppe Fanz & Neumayer | Marcus Bela Schmitt
Editorial department: Dr. Michael Barchet, Wolfgang Roth
Translations: Global-Text Fachübersetzungen, Heidelberg | Mark Woolfe, Jocelyne Abarca, Dr. Maria Carasi, Sebastián González Mohíno
Separations: EPS, Speyer
Printing: abcdruck GmbH, Heidelberg
Bookbinding: Josef Spinner Großbuchbinderei GmbH, Ottersweier

EDITION PANORAMA GmbH
G7, 14
D-68159 Mannheim

www.editionpanorama.com

A production by EDITION**PANORAMA**